City Centres, City Cultures

The role of the arts in the revitalisation of towns and cities

2nd edition 1991

Published by CLES
The Centre for Local Economic Strategies.
Alberton House,
St Mary's Parsonage,
Manchester M3 2WJ
061-834 7036

ISBN: 1-870053-23 0

Cartoons: Angela Martin © 1988
Printing: Manchester Free Press
Cover: Tattersall Hammarling & Silk, London

'It was always a limited inquiry. But it has brought me to the point where I can offer its meanings, its implications and its connections to others: for discussion and amendment; for many kinds of possible co-operative work; but above all for an emphasis — the sense of an experience and ways of changing it — in the many countries and cities where we live.'

Raymond Williams 1921-1988

Text: Franco Bianchini
Mark Fisher MP *(editor)*
John Montgomery
Ken Worpole *(editor)*

With many thanks for additional material and help to:
Crispin Aubrey
Peter Brinson
British American Arts Association
Mike Brook
Jean Carr
Geoff Hurd
Charles Landry
Su Maddock
Graham Markell
David Miller
Roland Miller
Dave Morley
Frank Mort
Geoff Mulgan
Robin Murray
Kath Nicholls
Russel Southwood
Michael Ward
Paul Willis

Franco Blanchini works at Liverpool University. He is the author of several articles and papers on the role of cultural policy in urban regeneration in Britain, Italy and the USA.

Mark Fisher is MP for Stoke on Trent Central and, since 1986, has been Labour's Shadow Minister for the Arts & Media.

John Montgomery was the research officer for SEEDS (the South East Development Strategy). He has published several articles and reports on retailing, the land market, the development process, and radical planning initiatives.

Ken Worpole is a freelance arts adviser and is also Policy Adviser to Mark Fisher MP.

Contents

Foreword

This book is about a growing problem, and a solution.

The problem is that trends in shopping and property development have tended to standardise and dehumanise our city centres. At the same time, the growing number of hypermarkets, out of town centres, retail warehousing and retail parks drains vitality and jobs from the town centres.

Since this book was first published in 1988, the developments it predicted have been seen to take effect. While part-time jobs have increased in retailing, they are now neither local nor convenient. They are often insecure, with worse conditions than those in traditional centres, isolated and poorly serviced by transport. Consumers too have lost out on the range of individual choice between local and specialist traders, faced with identical high streets wherever they go. The community, as a result, ends up with a demeaned urban environment.

This book is a positive contribution to the debate on the future of our towns and cities. It documents the solutions that have been pioneered by imaginative, creative local councils that bring the authority and traders together. It is about harnessing the ability of the arts industry to renew town centres. It also gives examples of good.practice from all over the country.

With the increasing importance of Europe in the UK economy, it is not irrelevant to look at the difference in cities such as Lucca in northern Italy, with streets closed to traffic and a dynamic night life in the centre, with some of our own cities. We do not want private shopping malls, closed to the public at night and policed by security guards and closed circuit television. A revived city centre with the public sector as the agency of change to promote diversity and choice is a libertarian, not an Orwellian, vision of the future.

This book brings together CLES' concerns with urban policy, the use of the arts in regeneration, changes in the retailing sector, and the prospects for service sector workers. We are republishing it not only as a contribution to the debate on the future, but as a guide for action for public and private investors.

Michael Ward

Director
Centre for Local Economic Strategies,
Manchester, March 1991

Introduction
by Gordon Brown MP

This book, which has influenced local authorities in cities as diverse as Brisbane and Barcelona, was first published only two years ago. At that time our cities were rapidly being carved up by the retailing revolution and a boom in property development. Within the space of a few years, the distinctive identity of many towns and cities seemed to be being replaced by a monolithic homogeneity.

Since the first edition of this book much has changed. The great retailing chains have been the first to bear the brunt of economic downturn, with a slump in property development following closely behind.

A great national debate about cities has started, sparked off by Prince Charles' interventions on architecture and fuelled by simmering discontent about the declining quality of life in many of our cities. It has become clear that a large majority are no longer prepared to put up with crumbling public transport, and with an ever starker contrast between private affluence and public squalor.

Unfortunately, there is no simple link between public demands and real outcomes. More than ever, decisions about the future of public spaces and the local environment are made in hopelessly undemocratic ways.

A recent MORI poll revealed that people do have ideas about what they want to see in their cities. Most called for open air cafes, evening facilities, weekend markets and playgrounds. Instead what they are generally getting are soulless, monofunctional developments with one zone for shopping, another for work. Far from becoming more sociable places, and more amendable to chance encounters, public life in cities is becoming more privatised and more segmented.

The same unwillingness to listen has permitted the poll tax and uniform business rate to be railroaded through, against the wishes of the majority. The new tax has devastated many of the small local shopkeepers who sustain the character of a city centre. Much of Stonegate, for example, the oldest shopping street in York, is now up for sale because of uniform business rates that are sometimes more than 30 times higher than previous rates. Even in prosperous Bath, dozens of shopkeepers have threatened a rates strike, while elsewhere thousands are disappearing as citizens and voters for fear of falling foul of the tax.

London's Canary Wharf development is another example of ill-thought out and undemocratic development. Without the necessary infrastructure and any thought as to how it can make a community, it is adding to the depressing failure of the Docklands development to create a city that is more than concrete and cars.

Meanwhile, the hundreds of new shopping centres that sprang up in the 1980s are rapidly becoming the tower blocks of the 1990s — unloved, underused, without character or care. They are proof of the failings of a private sector that doesn't work in partnership with the public sector and of the limits of an untrammelled free market.

Britain has also become an even shabbier place than it was two years ago. Our richest cities are unbelievably squalid, certainly by the standards of Europe. Milan, for example, spends nearly £1bn to keep its streets clean, with 6,000 employees clearing away 2,000 tons of litter each day. Paris too sees cleanliness if not as next to godliness then at least as an essential condition if it is to remain a pleasant place to live and a city able to attract industry. London, by contrast, stumbles on, spending a third as much per head on street cleaning as Paris, with an embarrassingly piecemeal approach to its environment, forced onto under-funded authorities struggling with privatisation and dissipated responsibility.

These are all economic questions as well as social ones. Unless we secure the quality of life in our cities, industry will move elsewhere. Unless we ensure high standards in restaurants, as, to take just one example, Oxford City Council has done by requiring those who want to be listed in its Good Food Guide to send staff on food handling courses, our tourism trade gap, £2,500 last year, will widen even further. Unless we improve the quality of public transport, investors will look elsewhere and hundreds of millions of hours will continue to be wasted in queues, delays and traffic jams.

The best cities are those that recognise that the private and public sectors work best together in partnership. This has been the lesson in the successful regeneration projects in the USA and Europe, and of Glasgow's renaissance which has seen annual tourism expand from 700,000 to 4m in a few years. Partnership also applies to public spaces. Cities and towns lose their coherence if private retailing is separated off from public buildings, town halls, swimming baths, parks and nurseries. A small but significant lesson can be learnt from Hounslow Council in West London, whose public library is sited in the middle of its shopping centre, seen by the shopkeepers as the hub around which the whole centre revolves.

A spirit of partnership will be essential if we are to find the imagination and care which the 1990s will demand. By the end of the decade cities may have even fewer cars, as environmental policies combine with road pricing schemes to pose a huge challenge not only for public transport but also for housing and shopping. People's habits are forecast to become more flexible, their demands on city centres more variegated. We can already see signs of this in the many pensioner's tea dances on weekday afternoons, in the remarkable fact that many of the most successful church services are now held on Wednesdays to attract shoppers, and even in the municipal swimming pools that rent themselves out for late-night parties.

City centres are important because they are the spaces we share. They symbolise the fact that we do live in societies and not as isolated individuals. If they decay, then there's a fair chance that people's sense of social responsibility and mutual obligation is also decaying. If people 'contract out' of any concern for their shared environment then there's a fair chance that they are also contracting out of any concern for the well-being of others.

Unbalanced development is economically unsound. It makes the whole less than the sum of its parts. This book helps to make the links between the quality of life and the economy: it points to the potential of the evening economy for regenerating the local economy, to the links between arts and industry and to the experiences of European cities where planning and the market work in tandem. This is perhaps the most potent argument, and the most damning indictment of many of the developments of the 1980s. For ill-considered commercial development fails even in its own terms. What it leaves a legacy of boarded-up shops, and dangerous, dirty empty spaces.

Gordon Brown MP is Shadow Spokesman for Trade and Industry.

Part I

The Arts Come to Town

The quality of life in our towns and cities has become, suddenly, a major political issue. Every day the newspapers report yet another inner-city initiative, urban redevelopment programme or planning disaster. Television documentaries abound on the conservation of historic buildings in our town centres. Everybody is talking about preserving the 'heritage', though whose heritage is not always questioned. Prince Charles' strictures on the excesses of some modern planning schemes, speculative property development and cut-price architecture are amongst the most controversial public statements of our time. Membership of environmental organisations now exceeds membership of all the political parties added together.

The social and economic fabric of our cities is coming under increasing pressure. Young people find they can no longer afford to live in the district where they were brought up. In some cases 'economic regeneration' simply means that working class people in rented council housing are forced out of their homes to make way for new high-earning owner-occupiers. Elsewhere, established town centres have been blighted by poor quality redevelopment, or by the disruptive effect of out-of-town shopping centres. High crime rates, worsening public transport services, badly maintained roads, pavements and street lighting, are all symptoms of this general picture. What can we do to start making things better?

The central claim we wish to make is that in many towns and cities the best strategic programme for improving the quality of life might well turn out to be based on developing a coherent and wide-ranging arts and cultural policy.

In the last ten years, public and commercial bodies have produced a bewildering array of schemes and initiatives to address the problems of urban centres. Mrs. Thatcher has appointed a Cabinet Minister, . Kenneth Clarke, as Minister for the Inner Cities. The Department of Trade and Industry has launched its Task Force and City Action Teams. The Department of the Environment has abolished the metropolitan counties, and with them their strategic powers in planning and economic development. Enterprise Zones and Urban Development Corporations have been established to replace local government powers with free market, deregulated solutions.

In the private sector, developers and building societies are moving in to transform the built environment of city centres with shopping malls, offices and car parks. Industrialists join together to promote Community Enterprise and Business Partnership schemes. Reports by agencies such as Shelter and the Child Poverty Action Group on the social consequences are joined by the Royal Institute of British Architects' on "Inner City Development". Among the most recent is one by the Office of Arts and Libraries on "The Arts in the Inner Cities", with numerous recommendations to sharpen the impact of the arts on the economic regeneration of cities, and with plentiful evidence of such arts-based initiatives already established.

What is inherently wrong with most of these reports is that they have identified only the 'inner city' as a focus of crisis. In fact throughout the UK almost every town or city centre is going through dramatic changes. Old buildings are pulled down to make way for new speculative office blocks and shopping precincts; large plastic and neon-lit facades are erected on top of Victorian and Edwardian shop fronts; and familiar local shops are displaced or driven out of business by rising rents, so that only building societies, banks and the multiple stores can afford a place in the High Street. Car traffic gets worse, and public transport in some places almost disappears.

Yet it is the town centre which gives most places their own unique and individual identity, often based on civic planning and public funding: the town hall, the library, a 19th century theatre, a town square, an ornamental garden, a municipal gallery, or in many places a church or market place. And this is of course how we think of cities in other countries too – as unique architectural aggregations of public buildings, boulevards, markets and so on – rarely as shopping centres.

The town centre is the physical focal point for the people who live and work there. Yet in many places it is being changed by market forces without any reference to the wishes of local opinion, whether in the form of elected councils or community groups. The big retailers and property companies have the money to spend, particularly in comparison with contracting local authorities, and therefore they have the final say.

What is at issue here is the gradual erosion of public space, or the 'civic realm' as it has often been called: that geographical and historical space in our towns and cities that properly belongs to the residents as a community, in the form of town squares, public gardens, street markets and meeting places. Today the building of new, enclosed shopping malls has literally taken that space away. What used to be public thoroughfares and streets and alleys have now been built upon by large shopping centres, which are closed at night and locked up. Increasingly people come into the town as isolated and individual consumers; rarely as active citizens or members of a civic community. In the short term this may seem not to matter. But in the long term if you take away people's sense of their own regional and local identity; as Glaswegians, Bristolians, Mancunians, East Londoners, as inhabitants of smaller towns each with its own unique past and heritage; and simply replace it with their identity as consumers, as Access card holders or Barclaycard shoppers, then this will have social repercussions of major and possibly frightening dimensions. What then will form the ties that bind us, as people, as communities, as citizens responsible for our own and each other's welfare?

Watch it all come down?

Our impulse to produce this pamphlet, trying to establish the links between arts and cultural policy, economic development and the revitalisation of our towns and cities, initially grew out of work some of us have been doing with local authorities on leisure policies. Despite rate-capping, the abolition of the Metropolitan County Councils, and the intense pressure on public sector spending, many local authorities have been trying to make their arts and leisure policies much more widely available to the populations they serve.

Yet time and time again arts and leisure officers find themselves fighting a rearguard battle to maintain a lively mix of activities in the town centre. 'The centre goes dead as soon as the shops close', 'People don't seem to want to go out at night anymore', 'It used to be very lively round here, but after they built the new shopping centre on the other side of the town, this area has gone completely quiet, are becoming typical comments.

This is why we have singled out 'the retail revolution' as deserving particular study and analysis (see Part II). For unless we understand the power of retailing — its positive as well as its negative implications — it will be almost impossible to plan any civic strategy at all. We have to understand the nature of the economic forces behind the credit boom, the frenetic programme of shopping centre speculation and development, and what long term implications these will have for both our environment and our social cohesiveness. And unless we are well prepared with counter arguments and schemes then it may well be that all our traditional notions of the value of civic cultures and integrated town centres will be buried under an avalanche of ill-thought out developments and bitter competition between neighbouring local authorities to grant planning permission for ever bigger hypermarkets and leisure parks. One can only knock down a public library or build over a market square once. In the demolition business there are no second chances.

We are also interested in the impact of retailing because many of its most sophisticated advocates have argued that shopping is *the* new leisure activity, and that it is through clothes and consumer goods that the majority of people now express their cultural identities and values. Hence such notions as 'festival retailing' and the 'theatre' of a shopping mall. We do not contest some truth in such ideas, but it is worth remembering that all the notions of colour, design and style expressed in modern retailing have been learnt in fact from the world of the arts and cultural expression. We must beware that the 'culture' of retailing does not end up destroying the culture of everyday life.

A wider definition of the arts

The civic identity of most towns and cities grew out of buildings associated with public cultural provision — the great Victorian town halls, public libraries, municipal art galleries, parks, civic theatres and concert halls. Today we live in an age in which what are defined as 'the arts' embrace a much wider range, including photography, film and video, radio and television, publishing, fashion and design. The strict demarcation lines between 'art' and 'design', 'serious' and 'popular' music, amongst many other divisions, no longer hold. And if in the end, our 'culture' is in fact everything that helps us make sense of the world we live in — from architecture or poetry, through the pleasure of music or dancing, the quality of our schools and child-care facilities to the feel of the streets we live in, then a 20th century cultural policy must embrace all this. This is why we believe that cultural policy can be the organising principle for the revitalisation of our towns and cities.

Employing a wider definition of the arts also involves a wider definition of the related services within which civic cultural policies can be developed. If public transport is bad locally, for example, and the town centre badly lit and poorly policed, then it is not surprising that many people, particularly women, will choose not to go out at night. A number of recent studies have shown that in many places, fear of assault or violence is a major factor for many people in deciding whether to go out in the evening. This affects young teenagers as well as elderly people. It is clear that cultural policy needs to be related to public transport, street lighting and policing policies.

But other factors play their part. If the local High Street is no longer a lively mix of shops, cafes, pubs, cinemas, dance halls, music venues and so on, but has been displaced by a single giant shopping centre with just the familiar names of the multiple stores, then it may be that cultural choice over a wide range of records, books, artists materials, crafts, hobbies and other specialist shops becomes an issue which should concern local government. This means having a policy on retailing. And if many of the local factories have closed down, and it becomes incumbent on the local authority to develop an economic strategy for the creation of new local industries, then cultural policy must be related to economic policy as well.

What we are arguing for, in the light of the complex social forces which currently beset our towns and cities, **is an integrated approach to revitalisation, one which combines the insights and disciplines of the various local government departments in one single strategic plan.** This is what we might term an 'holistic' approach to modern civic life, in which every detail of provision — whether public or private sector — is integrated into a coherent pattern, the whole being greater than the sum of the individual parts. This will also mean pioneering new ways for planners and developers, retailers and arts providers, councillors and the local people themselves to agree on policies to make our towns and cities better places in which to live and work.

How can the arts possibly lead economic development? One starting point is that the economic sectors of leisure, tourism, broadcasting, telecommunications and retailing are amongst the fastest growing in the modern economy. It is also true that jobs in the arts and cultural industries are some of the most cost-effective that can be generated by economic intervention, (though there are worries that some of the jobs, particularly related to tourism, have the same poor pay and conditions as the traditional services and catering sectors).

A city such as Glasgow, which has won the distinction of being nominated European City of Culture in 1990, has largely based its programme of urban regeneration on investment in the arts, museums, civic facilities and tourism. In 1984, 700,000 tourists came to Glasgow. By 1987, as a result of a concerted campaign of investment, marketing and promotion, this had risen to 4 million. The resultant prestige has been enough to attract increasing commercial investment in the city. And the same commitment to cultural investment, and consequently tourism, happened in Bradford, following the establishment there of the National Museum of Photography, the refurbishment of the Alhambra Theatre, and the revival of the Bradford Festival in 1987. Many of these developments also arose out of the initiatives of the city's Economic Development Unit.

In a number of American cities, leading strategists of 'downtown rejuvenation' have argued that arts-led investment is the most efficient way of beginning the process of raising morale and developing 'atmosphere' in what had become low status and moribund districts. As the Director of the US National Endowment for the Arts Program, Michael Pittas, has written: 'The arts demand centrality because their market is not so vast that they can be spread out, as shopping malls are. That makes for a natural affinity between housing the arts and revitalising the city centre. Commercial activities and the arts develop a synergy in these situations — together they generate more interest and support than each would alone.'

The Policy Studies Institute report on the economic impact of the arts in Liverpool published in 1987 clearly demonstrated that the arts are already major employers. In Glasgow some 8,000 people are directly employed in arts organisations — libraries, museums, theatres, dance and so on — and this does not include those working in our wider definition of the arts, for example broadcasting, fashion and design. The PSI report also showed that the 'multiplier' effect of each arts job was to create an additional 1.6 jobs in supplementary services.

When all the ''cultural industries'' are grossed together it becomes clear that in most urban centres, and even in many rural areas, they are a very substantial employer indeed and make a considerable contribution to the local economy. It is salutary to be reminded that nationally in the UK, the arts employ some 594,000 people — as against 485,000 people in the motor industry.

Despite this economic promise, the arts have traditionally played only

a minor role in local government policy. Often the arts officer — if there is one — has been located within a larger, sports-dominated 'leisure' service, which in turn has often been located within the most inappropriate committee structure — Parks & Cemeteries in some authorities, or under the Borough Engineer. This is no longer workable. For if it is the case, that in a number of UK towns and cities (as in Europe and America), economic regeneration and the restoration of a strong local civic identity *start* from cultural policy, then existing local government committee structures are badly in need of change.

Some cities have already realised the good sense of investment in the arts. Liverpool and Glasgow, for example, have long been aware that the arts and cultural industries have enormous economic development potential. In Liverpool, the Tate Gallery, the whole Albert Dock area and the expansion of the arts generally has been at the centre of the city's growing economic revival. It is likely that the Office of Arts and Libraries is the largest spending Government Department in the city after the DHSS. In Glasgow, the investment over the last five years in the MayFest Arts Festival has brought enormous sums of money into the city's economy and has been the central focus of a wider programme in the arts.

Other cities are recognising that the arts and cultural industries have an untapped potential in developing and reinforcing existing industries. Birmingham, for example, recently commissioned a consultative report on the potential of the audio-visual industry in the West Midlands. One key conclusion of this report was that the city's industries, both service and manufacturing, were having to spend huge sums of money each year outside the area on advertising, training and marketing films simply because the local audio-visual firms could not supply these needs.

For other cities, such as Newcastle-upon-Tyne, the arts play a wider, and more indirect part in the development of their inner city economy. Newcastle has found that investment in the arts — in galleries and theatres, for instance — is a key element in its programme for urban renewal. This programme involves huge retail development, bringing consumers, money and jobs into the inner city. And in this retail renaissance, the arts play a crucial role as an anchor element, improving the quality of the inner city environment. In the United States, Baltimore and other cities have discovered that not only does such arts investment broaden the range and variety of facilities that their inner city areas can offer but that, if properly developed, this can bring tangible benefits to the local authority in the form of lower inner city crime rates and less vandalism. Above all, investment in the arts can be a vital element in changing the image of a city or area, both attracting industry and new investment and holding on to key personnel and skills.

Glasgow's successful campaign, "GLASGOW'S MILES BETTER", specifically hinged around the improved quality of life in Glasgow after the City Council had invested so heavily in MayFest, the Burrell Collection, the Citizen's Theatre and the Third Eye Gallery. Cardiff has also seen the potential of using the arts and cultural industries to project the image of the city. In styling itself "CARDIFF — THE MEDIA CITY", it has stolen a march on other cities, such as Leeds, Manchester or Bristol, with perhaps an equally good claim. But the fact remains that there are over 4,500 people in Cardiff working in the broadcasting media, compared with the 11,000 working in the entire South Wales coalfield. This year, Bradford invested £100,000 in commissioning a new ballet from the London Festival Ballet — a new version of Swan Lake, to be choreographed by Natalia Makarova. This ballet will be in LFB's repertoire for at least five years, and will be performed all round the world, from Washington to Paris to Tokyo. In these cities, the Gala performances of this production will be in front of the chief executives, families, friends and relations of some of the largest corporations in the world, and the image of Bradford will be promoted in an original and effective way.

The arts and the built environment

So far, we have talked about the arts in urban centres in a relatively traditional sense. But if a cultural policy is to make any sense, it must also encompass the environment as a whole.

Partly as a result of the public debate opened up by the comments of Prince Charles, people have begun to question the relevance and humanity of much modern planning and architecture. However, architects should not be held directly to blame, since it is essentially the clients who determine the economic criteria within which any architect is allowed to work. Get-rich-quick commercial values have tended to mean 'get-built-quick' office blocks and housing estates. Those values must now be questioned, as the built environment is one of the most crucial factors in the quality of urban and rural life.

It is also time to recognise that some 95% of architects are men, but they are designing homes, hospitals, social services, shops and city centres to be used by people, of whom the majority are likely to be women. The feminist critique of modern planning and architectural values must therefore be taken seriously. Local authorities in particular can take a lead by both employing more women planners and architects, and making sure that there is full public consultation on new developments. Women have already proposed a number of ideas in the debate over civic planning and design, from the provision of child care facilities, through to new policing strategies and 'designing out crime' on estates. Yet developers and planners still seem to ignore most of these criticisms and suggestions.

New policies should also begin to turn the tide back against car-led planning philosophies, powerful though the road transport lobby is. Many towns and cities have been savagely attacked by crude and ugly road schemes cutting great swathes of noisy, polluted highways through town centres, leaving pedestrians to negotiate dark and dangerous subways or clamber up and over pedestrian bridges. Although shopping is now talked of as one of the great leisure activities, according to the National Consumer Council, "for many hundreds of thousands of consumers, it is little short of a nightmare. They are the low-income families, the single parent families, the elderly, the disabled and the non-car owners. They have to rely on wherever they can walk to or on public transport". An early 1980's study in Milton Keynes, for example, showed that 75% of housewives did not have access to the family car during the day; at the same time, bus passenger traffic declined nationally from 42% of all journeys in 1953 to just 8% in 1983.

There are other dangers too. The trend in modern retailing is towards 'niche marketing' — identifying particularly wealthy sections in the community and aiming the shopping facilities at them. This is why such groups as 'yuppies', 'dinkies' (double income, no kids) and 'woofies' (well off over fifties) have been identified. These labels may seem comic, but to the market researchers they are deadly serious target groups. Yet this kind of targetted retailing is at the same time missing other people out: the young and unemployed, the single parents, the elderly on state pensions. Where do they fit into the retail revolution? It increasingly seems they don't. Hence the proliferation of private security guards to move along any groups of young people who aren't spending, hence the exclusion of seating from shopping malls (a deliberate design feature to prevent the elderly or women with young children from sitting down and thus slowing down the rapidity of the crowd flow), and hence the lack of amenities such as toilets and informal meeting places. Along with the increasing use of video monitors mounted on public buildings and inside shops to observe the every action of the town centre crowd, it may seem that 1984 is just a little late. Will eventually only those with cars and credit cards be regarded as enfranchised citizens in the city centre?

At the same time, there is no doubt that the "community architecture" movement is here to stay. Popular involvement in architectural planning is one of the keys to bringing back a sense of identity between people and the towns and cities in which they live. In both Covent Garden in London and Wirksworth in Derbyshire — two of the best known experiments in regeneration of the past decade — popular planning and the involvement of local people in deciding what they wanted to see were major contributory factors to the success of these schemes.

In the case of Covent Garden, local residents acting with sympathetic planners and architects managed to get a proposed new redevelopment for offices and shops rejected by the Secretary of State for the Environment, and celebrated their 1974 victory with the first of what have become annual neighbourhood festivals. Subsequently, the district has been developed in close consultation with local environmental and neighbourhood groups to produce a living mix of residential accommodation, workshops, specialist retailing and leisure activities, including the now well established street entertainment and busking. Much is owed to the GLC administration between 1981 and 1986 for working so closely with community groups and funding many of the most exciting redevelopment projects. Today, Covent Garden is as synonymous with the popular arts as it is with opera, although the latest plans to redevelop the Royal Opera House threaten to impose a further ¼ million sq. ft. of office accommodation against the wishes of the local community.

The Wirksworth project demonstrated that the same principles of revitalisation could be employed in a small town of 6,000 residents, whose town centre had fallen into neglect through unemployment, poor quality local housing and the closure of a number of shops. Vandalism was high and young people complained of having nothing to do. A Civic Trust sponsored regeneration project was begun by establishing a detailed programme of consultation and, according to one account of the project: 'Eight years later the town had been transformed. Derelict buildings had been restored, the environment had been cleaned up, shopping had been improved, a range of new industries had been set up and there were new recreational and tourist amenities'.

The freedom of the streets

Many factors have contributed to the insecurity and fears of people — particularly women — about going out at night on their own or in small groups in our towns and cities. One root cause has been the growth of domestic entertainment such as radio and television. People simply do not spend so much time on the street anymore. And busy streets are invariably safer streets. It is worth remembering that three generations

ago the pubs were open all day long and street markets would often not close until midnight on a Saturday. Many fewer people had cars, and bicycles and public transport (and walking of course!) were the main methods by which people travelled in the cities.

The position today is very different but it is not beyond changing. In some European cities, for example — and as a result of public encouragement and investment — up to 30% of all city trips are made by bicycle. In the UK the figure is just 3%, not surprising since for years cycling has been ignored in transport planning, and cyclists have been excluded from traffic counts! Decades of governments obsessed with appeasing the road transport lobby have meant that public transport has been systematically downgraded and denied funds. This may benefit male businessmen, but not the rest of the population. In most European countries bus transport continues to expand; in the UK there has been a significant decrease.

As far as safety on the streets is concerned, women have been understandably angry that the police have only recently taken crimes such as rape and sexual assault as seriously as crimes against property. It is still a widespread attitude — not just amongst the police — that women who choose to go out on their own (or in small groups) at night, are somehow complicit in their own victimisation if something does go wrong. Hence the 'Reclaim the Night' demonstrations held in many cities by women protesting at their lack of freedom to feel safe on the streets at night. The police attitude that the streets are by definition dangerous places, and that people are only properly safe in their own homes, has also to be challenged. We would start from the premise that the streets should be safe for all people, and that going out at night does not itself constitute some minor form of criminality.

Liaison with the police on these issues is vital. Widespread consultation with local people, particularly voluntary organisations and women's groups, is vital too. Planners and architects should be told to prioritise issues such as street lighting, redesigning known places of danger to pedestrians and consulting with the police and transport bodies about mobility and safety at night. Also brought into the process should be local cinema and theatre managers, restaurant and pub owners, and all those involved in providing night-time leisure and recreation.

The evidence from American cities supports the notion that 'busy streets are safer streets'. Two letters written by American police chiefs to the editor of an American book on 'Local Government and the Arts', (L. Kreisbergs, New York 1979) are worth quoting in support of arts investment as a key ingredient in city revitalisation:

'We believe that arts activities can generally help reduce street crime. Both in those areas of Boston which have regular street cultural activities and in our theatre districts, there tends to be less crime during those times as the cultural events are on-going', Robert Wasserman, Assistant to the Police Commissioner, Boston.

'I do believe the great interest and participation in cultural events in San Jose is a factor in the low crime rates we enjoy.' Joseph MacNamara, Chief of Police, San Jose, California.

More generally, it has been found that crime is less frequent in 'mixed use' city centres, where daytime offices, shops and other places of work co-exist with housing, night-time retail outlets and places of entertainment. The importance of what has been termed 'natural surveillance' in relation, for example, to minor crime such as telephone kiosk vandalism has been confirmed by studies conducted in Sheffield. Good street lighting can also be important in reducing crime. In St. Louis, Missouri, the numbers of offences against individuals and car thefts decreased by 41% and 28% respectively after the city's street lighting was improved.

The special needs of young people

A priority for any policy of revitalisation must be the needs of young people. There is now growing up in our towns and cities a generation who have gone through school knowing that education doesn't necessarily lead to jobs, and who will probably have spent large periods of their most formative adult years — from 16-25 — out of work. Recent surveys of young peoples' attitudes also reveal that they have 'switched off' from politics, regarding all parties and all politicians with cynicism and even contempt.

It is not surprising, perhaps, if they throw their litter where they want, spray graffiti over bus shelter walls and shop-fronts, and sit in multi-storey car parks drinking themselves into oblivion. Coventry Council recently applied to the Home Office for permission to bring in a bye-law prohibiting the sale of alcohol in the town centre, as so many young people were spending their days drinking from cans and bottles in the shopping centre and creating a nuisance. If we do not devise active policies for involving young people in the political and cultural life of society, there is a danger of creating a missing generation.

Of course, local authorities in themselves cannot create jobs for young people overnight. But a strategy of provision for young people, that involves a large degree of consultation is essential. In Harlow New Town the council had the imagination to conduct a survey of local youth opinion on life in the town and young people's needs. Instead of hiring an outside professional agency to conduct the survey, they asked Harlow's best known punk band, The New Town Neurotics! The result was a very serious and thoughtful analysis.

Amongst the many needs expressed, an interest in getting involved in the growing musical and media culture was notably prominent. For young people, industry no longer automatically conjures up pictures of shipbuilding or machine-minding. They think of the growing media industries — of recording studios, pirate radio, making films and videos, making clothes and selling them, running record labels and so on. Harlow now has a lively rock music scene, with a local recording studio and a record label of its own.

This interest in the employment opportunities of the cultural industries also emerged strongly from a report by residents of the beleaguered Broadwater Farm Estate in Haringey after the 1986 riots. They wrote:

'We understand the regeneration of the inner cities as a global process of economic and social development, of cultural and spiritual growth. Youths from the estate have already accumulated rich experiences in different areas. Working for public or private contractors, they have gained invaluable knowledge and experience; working on their own initiative they have shown a strong gift and full-time commitment to establishing their own enterprises. A case in point is their inroad into the music and communications business.'

In Sheffield, the Council has backed the setting up of a large rehearsal room and recording studio complex for local bands, to which two established Sheffield bands, The Human League and The Comsat Angels, have linked their own recording studios. Money has also been put into the highly successful Leadmill arts and music venue just opposite, which attracts over 300,000 people a year. The Leadmill is not just a live music venue, there are music, dance and art workshops in the daytime, and it is managed and run by a co-operative, quite autonomous from the local authority or statutory youth service.

In St. Helens, the local authority has run workshops for young people in music and dance and encouraged those who have shown ability to set up their own dance companies or bands — and then helped them get paid work or recording contracts. Stirling Council is beginning to establish a relationship with another recording studio based project, Random Rhythms, where local bands can make demo tapes and even videos which can then be sent to mainstream or independent record companies. Brent Council, together with the near defunct GLC-backed Brent Black Music Co-operative, has also been the launching pad for many talented young black musicians and recording artists.

It is therefore likely to be through popular cultural forms such as rock music, dance, theatre, fashion, poetry, painting or design, that young people will find self-esteem and self-confidence, and in the process become more community conscious, rather than through a revival of 'Civics' lessons in schools. Most of the talented young black and Asian writers who are now coming to prominence in Britain have come up through community-based writers' workshops; the same is true of dance and drama. It is not surprising, therefore, that many local authorities are beginning to develop such appropriate strategies for young people, based on an *investment* in workshop provision and in the elementary, low technology forms of cultural production in the first instance, and with proper consultation with the young people themselves. 'Investment' is the right word, for these are the modern equivalents of the old apprenticeships, by which young people are given the skills and resources to earn their own living and then become independent people. All these things are possible, but it means local authorities developing dynamic economic and social policies; and that bring us back to the key role currently being played by retailing.

Part II

The Retail Revolution: Winners and Losers

One of the most significant new forces changing the face of our towns and cities is the "retail revolution", especially the shift to "out-of-town" shopping. Hardly a day goes by without a dramatically published proposal to build a new superstore, retail warehouse park, free-standing shopping centre or even an entire "Leisure Recreation Tourism Shopping" complex, often with offices thrown in for good measure. And every week we also hear of the hundreds of jobs that each new development apparently offers. Such claims are seldom realised.

Moreover, the effects that these new developments have on existing shopping areas, town centres and retail jobs locally are deliberately shrouded in mystery. Barristers and planning consultants argue over "trade diversion" figures and "impact assessments" at public inquiries, but no-one seems to be any the wiser. Meanwhile, local people and interest groups, who have to live with the consequences of the decisions made at these inquiries, often feel under-represented, isolated and intimidated. And yet the retail revolution has implications for us all, not least of which is the future of our town and city centres.

Why is there a retail revolution?

There are four distinct yet inter-related reasons why there is currently a retail revolution based on a movement away from high streets and town centres to larger and larger stores on the outskirts of town:

- market competition and corporate policy decisions within the retail sector;
- property development and speculation in the granting of planning permission;
- consumer segmentation and the credit boom;
- the adoption by large companies of new distribution and sourcing methods.

1. Competition

Within the retail sector there has been a growing concentration since the early 1960s, in the ownership and control of shop units especially in the food sector, but also in the sale of alcoholic drink, footwear and clothing. This process has intensified during the past eight years. Since 1982, for example, there have been twenty major takeovers, worth some £6.5 billion, in the British retail industry. In the end, this could mean the virtual domination of every sector of mass retailing by twenty or so companies. One effect of this is that the larger companies are now competing directly with each other for market share, within towns and across the country generally.

For example, in the food sector, supermarket chains have increased their market share at the expense of independents from 49% in 1966 to 65% in 1982, and are looking to a projected share of 80% by the mid 1990s. The top five multiples — Sainsbury, Tesco, Dee, Asda and Argyll — now have 52% of the grocery market, compared to 38% in 1985. This has been achieved by the development of bigger and bigger superstores and hypermarkets, by the use of branch computer systems and distribution centres on the motorway network, and the expansion of own-brand goods. The key element in the battle for market share, therefore, is the sheer bulk of turnover generated through the larger stores.

Thus, while there was only one superstore in Britain in 1967, by 1983 this had risen to 289. Some parts of the country, particularly the north of England, have been more affected than others, although intense development pressure is now being experienced in London and the South East. In 1985-86 alone, nationally, three of the large food multiples opened 70 new stores, but closed 232 existing ones usually smaller supermarkets in urban areas and on high streets.

A similar pattern emerges in the Do-It-Yourself and furniture/floor coverings sector. In 1984-85, around 30% of the furniture and floor coverings market was controlled by just eight multiples including Harris Queensway, MFI, Times and Allied Carpets. Ten years ago there were only 30 or 40 DIY warehouses in Britain; by 1987 there were around 600. One large multiple opens a new store every ten days. Again, much of this is accounted for by the development of retail warehouses and retail warehouse parks on the outskirts of towns. By 1990, it is estimated that 60% of the DIY market will be controlled by the multiples.

The boom shows no sign of slowing down. In Manchester, for example, there are currently proposals for *thirteen* new out-of-centre shopping centres. In the South East at least seven very large centres are proposed around the M25 motorway. Each of these would cost an estimated £200-300 million, Southampton City Council has even launched a campaign against out-of-town shopping, drawing attention to the fact that almost three times as much floorspace is proposed in South Hampshire as already exists in Southampton itself.

Nationally, in 1986 alone, 2.3 million square feet of out-of-town shopping centres were completed. A further 7.5 million square feet were under construction, 15 million square feet had planning permission, and a further 52 million square feet were proposed. At roughly 77 million square feet (if all of these schemes go ahead) this compare with a total of some 83 million square feet built in Britain since the early 1960s, most of it in town centres.

2. Property Development and Speculation

New shopping centres and large stores are proposed in one of two ways. A major store group — for example Tesco or Boots — may decide that it wants to trade from a new large store in a specified area. Usually, the group or company will then commission a construction company, property agents and architects to design the development, apply for planning permission and complete the building works. This is often referred to as occupier or tenant-led development.

However, shopping centres and stores are also built or commissioned, not by the retail companies themselves but by property development companies. These are speculative in the sense that the stores are proposed and built in advance of there being companies to occupy the new units. Developers often appoint letting agents to attract large multiples to locate in the new developments.

The success or otherwise of a new development depends on attracting these multiples and, if possible, a commitment by them to sign contracts for premises in advance of construction. If this can be achieved, then it becomes easier to secure finance for the scheme from pension funds, insurance companies and other funding organisations. As funding organisations are interested in the longer-term viability of the scheme and the stream of income received from rentals, they prefer occupants to be multiple companies rather than local independents. From the investor's point of view, the key element is the anticipated growth in the rents and premiums which retailers are prepared to pay for "attractive locations". At the moment, compared to high streets, out-of-town centres and stores provide spectacular returns.

Finally, shopping schemes are also proposed by landowners or companies with an option to purchase the land in question. Such companies often hold very few assets of their own, and may in fact be owned by one or two individuals. The key to this process is the granting of planning permission. Agricultural land may be valued, for example, at £13,000 per acre; while the same land with planning permission for a shopping centre is valued, overnight, at £1m per acre. On the larger sites, taking into account land for car parking, millions of pounds are at stake even before building work has commenced. In addition to these small specialist property companies, many manufacturing firms are selling old factory space to realise the large gains possible and moving production to new locations. Public sector landowners like Health Authorities, British Rail and the Water Authorities are also speculating in this way. With such large sums of money at stake, it is perhaps not surprising that, as Cambridge City Planner David Urwin put it, "developers are throwing about proposals for £50 million retail developments like confetti at a Mafia wedding."

3. Consumer Credit and Choice

We are often told that the retail revolution is consumer-led, that the retailers and developers are simply responding to new consumer preferences and higher disposable incomes. In a sense this is true, but it overlooks the fact that retailers spend considerable amounts of money on advertising in order to create new demand for products and goods. Certainly, shopping is for many people now an expression of choice, fashion, style and personal income, with shops being compared on nuances of quality, design and image.

Much of this spending, however, is fuelled by an unprecedented growth in consumer credit since the relaxation of hire purchase controls in 1982. Retail sales continue to reach record levels, particularly in household goods, clothing and footwear, but there are worrying signs that consumer credit, particularly retail charge cards, are a major source of bad debt in Britain. The incidence of people being ensnared by loan sharks as they attempt to clear their debts is dramatically on the increase.

The new consumerism demands greater choice, whether in terms of the range and quality of products on offer or their convenient accessibility (which usually means car access). It is for these consumers that the new shopping centres and stores are built: people with cars, freezers, higher disposable incomes, consumer credit and owner-occupied houses to improve. A substantial minority are not in this position:

> "The have-nots — the old, the unemployed, the young mums on a budget — have little access to credit, except the expensive HP kind. No one's investing in new shops for them," Jean Carr, The Observer, 28 June 1987.

Indeed, the shops on which the "have-nots" rely most are often victims of the retail revolution as they suffer the consequences of new large stores opening on the edge of town and diverting their higher-spending customers. Many of the large companies, especially the food multiples, are closing smaller supermarkets as part of a corporate policy of pushing higher volumes of turnover through larger stores. The stores being closed are usually in town centres and high streets. Many people then, have little consumer choice, and are directly suffering the effects of disinvestment from high streets and local shopping areas.

4. Distribution and Stock Control

The new large stores and shopping centres are usually located on or near major road interchanges. This allows them to handle higher volumes of goods and more extended product lines, and to attract higher spending car-borne shoppers. It also allows the companies to benefit from economies of distribution, increasingly based on the motorway network. Sainsbury, for example, channels over 80 per cent of its turnover through central warehousing.

There are numerous advantages for the retailer in centralising the delivery and distribution of supplies and goods. These include a strengthening of the retailer's negotiating position with suppliers, and higher labour productivity in goods handling due to bulk deliveries, reductions in the level of stock at any one time, lower storage costs on less expensive warehouse sites and the release of storage space in shops for sale and display. Thus the major retailers can exercise considerable economic control over their suppliers and, through

computerised stock control and buying, can alternate sourcing of
supplies from area to area and even internationally.

Who are the losers?

To summarise then, there are several reasons why we are witnessing a
boom in out-of-town shopping developments and proposals. From the
retailer's point of view, large stores are a key element in the competition
for market share and productivity. They attract the higher spending car-
borne shoppers, are cheaper to build than similar centres in the centre
of towns, can accommodate more goods and generate higher
turnovers, and they offer a chance to plan from scratch. For developers,
vacant sites on the edge of towns are easier and less expensive to build
on, while landowners and property companies are able to submit
development proposals on virtually any plot of land, in the absence of
any coherent planning framework. And the consumers prefer out-of-
town centres because they appear to be easier to get to, are well-
designed and more secure, with controlled environments and internal
policing, and because they are single-trip destinations — an outing for
the day.

   So if the retailers, the consumers and the developers all benefit from
this revolution, who exactly are the losers? The statistics speak for
themselves. In 1961 there were 580,000 shops in Britain; by 1982 this
had fallen to 332,000, a drop of 43%. There were 278,000 food stores
in 1961, but only 115,000 in 1982, a loss of 60%. Most of the casualties
have been small, independent self-employed traders. In 1961 there
were some 590,000 working proprietors in Britain; only 300,000 remain
today.

   Particularly badly hit have been the grocers, greengrocers, smaller
high street and local centre supermarkets, and most recently, butchers
and bakers. *Business Monitor* figures reveal the disappearance of 10,000
household goods stores and 3,000 hardware stores between 1982 and
1984 alone. In the food sector, some towns are now virtually dominated
by one or two large multiples operating from edge or out of town
locations, and as trade is diverted to these stores from existing shops,
those who don't have access to a car are left relying on stores which
themselves are feeling the effects of competition. Following the
opening of a hypermarket in Neasden, for example, an existing
supermarket experienced a 25% loss of trade.

   In turn, this can produce a cumulative effect, so that, with the closure
of a supermarket or a small Marks and Spencer's, those who are able to
do so, or can afford to, switch to other shopping centres altogether,

encouraging further decline. In a country where already 80 per cent of the population live within a 15-minute drive of at least two shopping centres, the high street and the town centre — with their jumble of architectural styles, congestion, limited car parking, often dirty and windswept appearance, and with shops all the wrong shape and size for modern retailing — are an increasingly unpopular option.

So more shops close, to be replaced by banks, building societies, travel agents and fast food shops. And in the wake of this town centre "disintegration" follow vandalism, violence and crime:

> "A man disabled with multiple sclerosis was attacked by five men in the centre of Oxford on Saturday afternoon — the 13th outbreak in a wave of violence this year which is alarming police. A local newspaper, the Oxford Star, fears the heart of the city is becoming a 'no go' area for peaceful people." *Guardian*, 6 May 1987.

There is an added dimension to these changes — of standardisation. As more and more market share is controlled by the large multiples, and as increasing numbers of small shopkeepers leave the industry, for whatever reason, the tendency is for shopping centres throughout the country to look exactly the same. Most town centres now have a Marks and Spencer's, Boots, Woolworth, Mothercare, Currys, Dixons, Rumbelows, Saxones, BHS or Littlewoods, Next or Principles, Top Man or John Kent. It is often very difficult for independent, locally specific traders to let space in a new development, partly because of relatively high rents and partly because they have neither the corporate back-up or assets to guarantee, to the leasing agent, a secure rental stream.

As high street or shopping centre rents escalate, independent retailers are in turn forced into side streets or areas of 'secondary' or even 'tertiary' retailing. In many towns and cities this may work reasonably well, but in others — especially new towns or city centres which have been subject to massive redevelopment — the secondary sites may well not even exist. This means that consumer choice is then usually restricted to the multiple retailers. Hence the increasingly familiar cry that 'every High Street looks the same'.

New jobs or new jobs for old?

Developers argue that the new shopping centres and stores provide much-needed employment. This begs the question, however, of whether these jobs replace or displace old ones. and whether they really are appropriate to local employment need and the national economy.

In fact, the long term employment trends in the retail sector are towards the displacement of full-time by part-time work, resulting in the loss of some 900,000 full-time equivalent posts between 1961 and 1984.

During the 1980s there appears to have been a small increase in the *numbers* of people employed in retailing, but the new jobs have largely been part-time, many of them on contracts for less than 16 hours per week. While part-time employment is a potentially liberalising opportunity, especially for those with caring responsibilities, the significance of part-time work in the retail sector is increased productivity through the use of computerised check-outs and stock control, labour deskilling and the casualisation of, for example, shelf-filling.

Retailing also remains the third lowest paying industry in the British economy. The 1985 New Earnings Survey revealed that only gardeners and farmworkers were paid less than male sales staff, while full-time women staff on average receive between 70 and 80 per cent of the male rate. Part-time women receive even less; the average gross weekly earnings of part-time females with Wages Board agreements in 1984 was £38-40. The true picture is likely to be even worse, as the New Earnings Survey is a one per cent sample of those who pay national insurance. Many part-time women and young people working in the retail trade do not.

In addition to this, those on contracts for under 16 hours per week (of whom there has been a dramatic increase) are denied protection over unfair dismissal, redundancy pay, maternity pay or time off to look for work. Unless they have five years' continuous service, they have no legal rights to a minimum period of notice, written reasons for dismissal or a written statement of terms and conditions. With the out-of-town boom, many workers also face longer, more expensive and potentially more dangerous (travelling alone late at night) journeys to and from work.

The effect of this increase in part-time working is to cut wage levels and hours worked, undermine employment conditions and protection, and decrease the number of full-time staff, particularly adults. Jobs for young people, however, are largely confined to YTS and other government training schemes (paying under £30 per week). The shopworkers, trade union, USDAW, reports that YTS trainees are often obliged to work unpaid overtime and on public holidays, while cost-cutting has resulted in almost constant under-staffing in many stores, particularly superstores and retail warehouses.

However, shop working need not necessarily be low paid, de-skilled, monotonous, repetitive or exploitative. On the contrary, retail employment could and should be convenient, attractive in terms of developing skills and working with the public; flexible in positive ways; provide a pleasant working environment; rewarding in terms of developing social skills and product knowledge; and should be recognised as a valuable occupation. In considering future strategies for shopping areas and town centres, account must be taken of factors such as pay levels, health and safety, employment rights, training needs, store location and layout design.

Public space and 'the new enclosures'

One of the most insidious effects of the development of many town centre shopping centres is that what used to be public space becomes privatised. Shopping centres built on the site of old houses and streets are often locked up at night and people discover that old popular thoroughfares have suddenly became private property. These are 'the new enclosures'.

One of the worst examples of this privatisation of public space is in Basildon, where the Commission for New Towns (CNT) has almost complete control over large sections of the town centre. Some of this influence is vested in the Basildon Town Centre Management Company, the shareholders of which are private town development companies alongside the CNT. But this organisation, astonishingly, does not include Basildon District Council, and thus the local elected authority is formally excluded from participating in the planning or development of these sections of the town.

As a result, a rigid division has developed within Basildon's town centre whereby one end of the main open plaza incorporates nearly all the public facilities — council offices, rates department, library, advice centre, theatre and arts centre — and the other end is where the glamorous new shopping centre has been built. The complete separation of public and private means that the users of each sector feel they belong to two different worlds. In practical terms, people who are out shopping may never have to go near the theatre or library — a classic example of a wasted opportunity.

Surely it would have been much better to integrate the public and private facilities where they complement each other — for instance, through the notion of a ''cultural quarter'', where public swimming pools, gymnasia, theatre, arts centres and sports halls co-exist with private sector shops, wine bars, cinemas, night clubs and so on. Yet in Basildon it seems, worse is yet to come. For a private development company is now planning to put a roof over the whole of the town centre. Once that is achieved, a large part of the centre will be locked up at 8pm! This could have a catastrophic effect on the newly built Towngate Theatre and Arts Centre.

The design cycle

In conventional property terms, the investment cycle for retailing property has been directly linked to the length of the lease; in the past about 21 years. This has allowed the freeholder to capitalise the building and at the end of the cycle to renew and redesign the building if necessary.

The economics of the 21 year cycle imply a given level of rent. However, because of increasing pressures in the market-place, the investment renewal cycle is being pushed down from 21 years towards 15. This means that unless the developer can put buildings up more cheaply, or other costs are reduced, the pressure to put up rents also increases. The end result is cheaper buildings and higher rents — in the long term bad news for the quality of the built environment and for local retailers.

In addition to this, major changes in the style of shopping and retailing have induced other pressures on rents and overheads — notably the costs of redesigning the shops (or 'retail environments' as they are increasingly called) at ever greater levels of frequency in order to keep up with the competition. As retailers such as Next, Richards, Alias and Benetton compete with each other for custom through 'state of the art' design, so the expense of competing becomes increasingly prohibitive. Whereas a generation ago a major retailer might only redesign a shop or department store once every 10 or even 15 years, today some shops are redesigning their interiors every two or three years. The independent retailers can't compete and even the multiple chains are having difficulty. In times of crisis, when you can no longer afford to keep up with your competitor, there remains only one other choice — buy them out! Thus competition in the end leads to increased monopolisation.

Which, in a sense, brings us full circle. For one of the advantages that the out-of-town movement appears to have over traditional town centres and high streets is that developments are designed from scratch to maximise efficiency in distribution and stock control, and to provide more attractive environments for shoppers. This ranges from the careful co-ordination of colour schemes and displays, through food courts, cafes and childrens' play areas, controlled temperatures and lighting, to leisure themes and matching muzak. All of this is combined with ease of movement within the new developments; spacious aisles, ramp access for prams, trolleys and wheelchairs, escalators and level floors. Thus functional design is carefully researched to provide the 'right' mix of comfort, convenience, accessibility and ambience.

Against this sort of competition and the emphasis on design, many town centres and High Streets appear badly co-ordinated, windswept, congested, dirty, drab, noisy, cluttered and visually muddled. The British Council of Shopping Centres has recently produced a report, 'Managing the Shopping Environment of the Future', which argues that town centres *must be managed as single entities* if they are to remain competitive and continue to meet their traditional social roles. The role of good design, they argue, is vital. Among their suggestions are co-ordinated transport provision and much greater accessibility, pedestrianisation, landscaping and street furniture, control over and better design of shop frontages, proper maintenance and street cleaning, the provision, cleaning and supervision of public conveniences, the provision of rest areas, cafes and restaurants, and better marketing and information on local heritage and culture.

This is all very well and to be commended. What it lacks, however, is a clear analysis of why so many town centres are under threat, or fail to achieve their potential as social and cultural entities. In our view, town centres must be revived as cultural, artistic and civic centres — as well as simply shopping and commercial centres. Good design will be an important feature of this, but not a solution in itself. For the problems faced by town centres are as much economic and political as physical and environmental.

Why is there no control?

If the above analysis is correct, then why is the retail revolution — with all its attendant problems for employees, consumers and the wider public — being allowed to proceed unchecked. The answer, put simply, is government policy, and the drive to de-regulate markets, privatise public services, remove the 'burden' of planning controls, and strip local authorities of their property ownership.

Nicholas Ridley, the current Environment Secretary, has said he believes that local authorities should not own land, enterprises, houses or other buildings, the public ownership of which he chararacterises as 'municipal socialism'. Yet the strategic role of local authorities to plan and regulate land use developments has largely been the reason why our towns and cities retain what coherence and individual identity they have.

The Department of Environment has produced just one short

statement on the subject. This starts encouragingly enough by stating that growth in retailing "generates opportunities both for new forms of retail development and for the modernisation and improvement of existing town centres". It continues to flirt with tautology by observing that "Town centres need to maintain their diversity and activity if they are to retain their vitality, but the range and variety of shops and services will change, as they have always done, in response to changing conditions". But at least these truisms seem well-intentioned.

Doubts about the usefulness of government thinking begin when the Secretary of State confidently asserts that it is not "necessary to attempt a detailed calculation or forecast of retail growth". Yet without the factual base of quantitatively assessing what is happening. It is virtually impossible to understand the likely qualitative impact on the social or cultural life of our city centres. There is similar confusion about the relationship of transport policies to these developments. The Secretary of State recognises that the needs of those without cars, who are in a majority in many cities, "must continue to be catered for". But his proposition that developments should be accessible to non car owners "where possible" scarcely tackles the problem, while the argument that city centre traffic congestion will be *helped* by taking heavy car-borne shopping requirements out of centres is a nonsense. The prosperity and cultural diversity of city centres is unlikely to be helped if traffic is reduced simply by attracting people elsewhere.

Beyond these specific inadequacies, the statement displays no understanding whatsoever of the social or cultural impact of these developments, or the role that the arts and cultural industries could play. Without that wider context, and without any form of concerted strategy or support for local authorities' planning powers, Mr Ridley's recognition that there could be dangerous cumulative effects from large developments, and his acceptance of the need to maintain the vitality of city centres, ring somewhat hollow.

William Waldegrave, a junior minister at the Department of Environment, has also stated that '... it is not for land use planning to dictate that any particular kind of development, or any particular kind of retailing, is a Good thing or a Bad thing in itself'. Many people — and not just 'municipal socialists' — would disagree. The planning profession itself is deeply worried about deregulation and the notion that, as one planner put it, 'the forces of supply and demand will regulate the location of shops and services'. Architects and designers are worried too, particularly where large areas of redundant land are becoming available for redevelopment — as in docklands and waterfront sites. Piecemeal development would be likely to end up in an uncoordinated miscellany of architectural styles and unrelated mixes of shopping, residential, retail and industrial sites.

Private developers have often promised to local authorities — in return for planning permission — such concessions as low-cost housing or industrial workshops. But these have been the first parts of the developer's plans to be jettisoned at the sign of a hiccup in the rate of profitable return. In how many private seafront marina developments or lakeside housing schemes of the 1970s did the social housing ingredient actually get built? This is not to say that private developers should be excluded from any role in regeneration — simply that they should not be given the leading or strategic role. As the architect Ralph Erskine has aptly put it: 'Private enterprise is good at getting things done, but not good at choosing what to do.'

As we have seen, the market and the private sector competing in isolation tends on the one hand to provide too much — shopping centres are in favour one month, hi-tech factories the next — whilst on the other a whole range of social needs and preferences are never met. These unacknowledged needs include, for example, access to town centres and shops for *all* the community, not just those with cars — or indeed the right, against the background of private security police, to be in the town centre at all.

Part III

Reviving the Cities

In this concluding part we look at the variety of strategies which local authorities and others can employ to ensure a healthy mix of activities in our towns and cities — particularly in the centres — making them lively and attractive places for all sections of the community. And as we have already emphasised, we believe that it is essentially a *cultural* policy which can best be the organising principle behind the revitalisation of civic life.

No one single strategy will suit every town and city in the UK. Each place should endeavour to create its own individual policy for urban renewal. It is for this reason that we suspect the present policies for urban regeneration to be rigidly dogmatic — with every Urban Development Corporation pursuing the simple formula of one hypermarket, one yachting marina and one garden festival (plus some private middle management housing) Surely there aren't enough boats to fill all the marinas currently planned? In the same light, not every town and city can have its own telecommunications industry, opera house, professional ballet company, national museum, film studio and record industry. But every town should be able to develop something of national interest that is unique, and based on local traditions and culture. Bigness is not everything; diversity and choice are more important.

Bradford Council paved the way for this approach when it successfully established the National Museum of Photography in the town, one of the first national museum centres outside London. Glasgow built much of its current cultural policy around a stunning new gallery for the Burrell collection of fine arts. Sunderland Council has refurbished the Empire theatre as a first step in bringing back life to the city centre and creating a stronger local identity; Cardiff has proclaimed itself 'Media City' as part of its encouragement of the audio-visual industries; Birmingham now sees itself as an international conference and exhibition centre; Edinburgh is famous for its international arts festival; Sheffield for its commitment to young people and the development of an indigenous music industry; the Royal Exchange Theatre has helped put Manchester on the international theatre map. But even in smaller towns, arts provision can be the focus of town centre renewal — as the theatre has been in Guildford, and hopefully will be in Basildon. In Wakefield, a strong commitment to the public arts, high quality pedestrianisation and the refurbishment of the Opera House have all helped boost the self-confidence of the town. In Bristol, the two arts centres down by the quayside, the Arnolfini and the Watershed, led the regeneration of that part of the city; Manchester's support in the creation of a Chinatown district helped another small area of the city to find its identity.

Town and community festivals have also been important in identifying established and new communities. Notting Hill now has its annual Carnival; London's Soho celebrates the Chinese New Year; Birmingham and Southampton both run annual film festivals; North Tyneside has invested in an annual festival set around its traditional Fishquay; Mayfest in Glasgow has become one of the most exciting festivals in Europe.

But if local authorities recognise the potential of cultural regeneration, even if they can develop strategies sufficiently in advance of development schemes to retain control of them, and establish new and productive relationships with outside agencies and the independent sector; there are still many problems that must be addressed.

Problem One: Contending with Government

In the immediate future, any cultural industries strategy may well have to be implemented against a background of government hostility, in particular in the form of political deregulation and financial restraint. It is especially likely that the relaxation of planning powers that has been a feature of the last eight years will continue, with the requirement to put services out to competitive tender extended to apply not only to sports and leisure centres as in the 1988 Local Government Bill but also to arts centres and even public libraries. The opportunities offered by Section 52 of the Town and Country Planning Act, which allows for planning gains may well be closed or tightened.

Above all, central government is certain to continue its stranglehold on local authority finance. This year (1988), for example, huge cuts are being required of councils which are to the fore in developing cultural strategies. Manchester is being forced to reduce spending by £110 million or 26% of its total budget. Camden, with one of the best established arts budgets in the UK, must cut £44 million, 28% of its total budget, from which cultural expenditure on over 100 voluntary organisations has not escaped unscathed.

Problem Two: Private Sector Pressures

Reclamation and regeneration of city centre sites invariably leads to inflated land values. This, in turn, tends to inhibit the use of such sites for any public, non-commercial cultural use. In the USA, "Mixed Use Development" projects, combining several revenue-producing uses, such as retail, office, hotel, residential and recreation, have been pioneered, and provide encouraging results for commercial developers. However, the Urban Land Institute in Washington warns that the use of returns on capital investment from such projects is slow, acting as a further disincentive to many developers, and tightening the economic context in which decisions are made.

Some managing companies take the view that adjoining cultural amenities such as a public library, gallery, museum or media centre, attract potential customers and hold them in the area longer. The National Museum of Photography in Bradford is now attracting over 800,000 visitors a year of whom 40% live more than 25 miles away. They provide a new consumer market for retailers, and it is no surprise that Bradford City Council is now developing the shopping district next to the museum to exploit this potential.

However, other retailers, such as the newsagent and leisure multiple, W.H. Smith, seem less convinced about such a coincidence of interest. For them, an easy and convenient mutuality of interest between retailing and arts and leisure provision is unlikely to exist. They argue that the commercial pressures on multiple retailers — increased competition, turnover, growing advertising and marketing costs — are so acute that other considerations, such as the cultural use of city centres, providing a variety of amenities, are simply a distraction from the harsh imperatives of showing a return on development costs. They do not oppose the idea of mixed developments so much as insist that the needs of "professional" retailers must come first. The public can be single-minded about seeking either shopping or cultural activity, but not both. Any distraction from being a customer sets alarm bells ringing.

Shop frontages are one further source of contention between retailers and planning authorities who seek to improve the visual quality of their city centres. For retailers, the design of their shop frontage is a key factor in attracting customers. If it has no impact, they have no sales. Not only are companies investing hugely in this presentation of their image, but they also are changing that image more frequently. In a highly competitive market, there is an obvious need to catch the consumers' eye with immediate colour, lighting or materials. When such frontages are vying with each other within shopping malls whose frontages are visually internal, there are seldom problems. But in the development of established city centres, the needs of the retailer can be sharply at odds with the desire of local people to retain the identity and character of their city, particularly when buildings are of architectural coherence or merit.

Problem Three: Day and Night Economies

All the above problems presuppose that the activities and economies of retailing and cultural activities in our city centres coincide in time. Often they don't: one operates most frequently in the morning and afternoon, the other at night. For museums, galleries and libraries, a coincidence generally occurs, although many of them would like to remain open in the early evening to attract people after work. But most of the performing arts and cinemas concentrate on evening performances. In doing so they nonetheless sustain restaurants, wine bars, pubs and clubs to service their audiences.

The one line between these day and evening economies can be cultural retail activities such as book and record shops. The success of Waterstone's bookshops and Virgin and Tower record shops in staying open until 9pm, or even later, is encouraging. In Covent Garden and its surrounding streets, the two economies merge well into the evening. But such solutions are only viable where there is a sufficient concentration of people to make the later hours, with their higher staffing costs, profitable.

Problem Four: Duplication

Finally, there is the danger of duplication. Cultural development of city centres will be less effective if the activities and facilities are duplicated in a nearby city. It is vital that there is co-operation between authorities to avoid this.

It should be emphasised that the integration of the arts and cultural industries in the economy of the inner city offers no guarantee of success. Ultimately, each city has to tailor a strategy of its own to reflect the lifestyles, identity and expectations of its people. But where investment in the arts has been used as an anchor element of regeneration, as in Glasgow or Newcastle, or in Baltimore in the United States, the success is marked both by the enhanced quality of life and in the boost to jobs and the economy.

Responses

The retail revolution undoubtedly presents exciting opportunities to establish new arts projects in city centres. At the same time, it is physically transforming the hearts of our cities. The centre of Newcastle-on-Tyne, around Eldon Square, for instance, has had its buildings restored and its streets reshaped, while Birmingham is just embarking on a £1 billion redevelopment scheme which will involve the demolition of the Bull Ring. These changes will determine not just the shape and facilities of our city centres for the next generation, but their aesthetic appearance and architectural quality.

The Prince of Wales, in his speech at the Mansion House (December 1987), criticised post-war architects and planners for building "scientifically concerned slabs" in spaces where "nothing but the wind plays". His remarks referred specifically to Paternoster Square and the area around St. Paul's Cathedral, but they could have applied equally well to the residential tower blocks, offices and civic buildings which dominate many cities and give their centres such a bleak and dispiriting anonymity. Many would take issue with his implied preference for an aesthetic that recreates the styles of the past, rather than attempting to find a contemporary architectural language, but few would disagree with his criticism of existing planning laws, which are devoid of any aesthetic criteria and have so often been applied ineptly by both central and local government.

Most crucially, this speech recognised that higher standards in the quality of our built environment cannot be achieved solely by private developers and financiers operating in a free market economy. The public sector has got to be involved, through better national planning legislation and through local authorities which develop wider-ranging and more thoughtful planning strategies and which then consult more widely with the public before implementing them. For a start, we must agree on some basic principles which can be broadly subscribed to by planners and developers; by architects, artists, craftspeople and landscapers; by local and national politicians; and by the general public.

First, we should recognise that architecture, landscaping and the built environment are omnipresent and therefore the most accessible of all the arts. Our inability to avoid them ensures that they have the greatest physical impact, for good or ill, on the quality of public life. They both embody and create the cultural identity of a city, determining its atmosphere and its relationship with individuals, even simply through the height of buildings or the width of streets. But the quality and quantity of transport, the range of facilities on offer and the existence of somewhere attractive to sit and meet friends will also determine how much a city centre is used. In short, consideration of the built environment should not be confined simply to the quality of the buildings and surrounding spaces but must encompass the people who live and work there.

Above all, we should realise that improved strategies for investment in the built environment make economic sense. With even medium-sized shopping malls costing over £50 million, there is a tendency among both developers and local authorities (who stand to benefit from much needed increases in rates and often in a share of rents) to wish to maximise office accommodation or the revenue from retail outlets. Such considerations allow little space for elements or services which do not and cannot generate such income. However, the experience of mixed-use environments in the United States shows that a more balanced development portfolio can perform in the medium term as well as, or even better than, a development that seeks only to maximise short term profits.

Indeed, many UK cities are beginning to recognise that 'non-profitable' cultural investment actually *promotes* economic growth. This is most easily seen in the examples of Glasgow and Bradford already discussed, but it is equally true of the aesthetic quality of a city's architecture, as Birmingham has recognised. In seeking to create a new cultural image for the city internationally, Birmingham City Council is promoting the visual quality of its £1 billion city centre redevelopment by means of European-wide architectural and design competitions.

Recognising the importance of architecture and the built environment is a necessary first step, but achieving real improvements will not be

possible unless we release the talents and imagination of individual
artists, crafts people and architects. Since the war, both the involvement
of and investment in such artists has been at a low level in the UK.
However, there appears at last to be a recognition that the good
practices which have been developed elsewhere, such as in Holland
and the USA, could be adopted here, not least the idea of "Percentage
for Art" schemes.

Percentage for art?

The British designer Theo Crosby wrote recently that 'the construction
industry is desperate for skills and intelligence, and our buildings are
universally condemned as dull and inadequate... Our need is largely for
re-training. We have thousands of perfectly unused artists. They need to
be taught how to acquire the skills that are now being demanded
through the change in architectural style. Ornament, decoration, skills
in finish and detail are once again thoroughly respectable and in
demand'. If, as Crosby asserts, 'one high street or shopping centre looks
exactly like another', then there is an urgent need to redress the
balance by giving every town a distinctive visual geography of its own.

Crosby advocates the adoption of 'Percentage for Art' schemes, the
basic premise of which is that a percentage of the construction costs of
a building or development are put aside to improve the aesthetic
quality of the project. Philadelphia pioneered such a scheme in 1958.
Since then, 22 states and 88 cities in the USA have followed suit, usually
with a 1% limit, although Dallas specifies 1.5%.

The details of these schemes vary, with different sorts of
development or categories of building being exempt in different cities.
Los Angeles has a particularly flexible system, whereby 40% of the 1%
is placed in a Downtown Art Trust, which invests in cultural projects of
all kinds for the benefit of the community — from landscaping to arts
festivals to theatre in education. Other schemes are more
straightforward, with the percentage being dedicated to specific works
of arts, such as sculptures, murals or paintings, which are incorporated
in the building concerned. The potential weakness of the Percentage
for Art approach, if poorly implemented, is that it amounts to 'lipstick
on the gorilla' of a building which is itself ugly or slipshod. To work
effectively, Percentage For Art cannot be conceived solely in decorative
terms, but as an integral part of a development in which artists and
architects have been involved from the earliest stages.

The importance of such planning extends well beyond the individual
building or project. If a city is to ensure a coherence to its
developments, it is vital to have, in advance, an overall strategy that

incorporates aesthetic style and quality at the heart of the planning brief, and that this is pursued at all levels — from architectural detail and furniture such as street signs, seating and railings up to the wider context of roads and transport.

There are encouraging signs that these approaches are beginning to be adopted in the UK. The local authorities in Edinburgh, Birmingham, Sheffield, Hereford and Worcester have all approved Percentage for Art schemes in principle, while Swindon, Belfast and Newcastle-on-Tyne have, for some years, demonstrated genuine concern for the aesthetic quality of their cities without formally adopting a percentage policy. This work is being particularly promoted by architectural pressure groups such as Acanthus and Art and Architecture, and has given rise to the establishment of at least six consultancies.

Whatever form these schemes take, it is certain that there will be little improvement in our architectural environment without there first being a change in national planning legislation, in strategic planning policies by local authorities, and by greater consultation and partnership with the local communities concerned. What is worrying is that the present government is intent on going in the opposite direction, by an obsessive hostility to local government finances and powers, by weakening the planning laws in key areas through the creation of Urban Development Corporations, and by its determined failure to recognise the significance of the retail revolution or the importance of cultural investment. A classic example of this was the report (by Paul Collard) commissioned by the Office of Arts and Libraries in September 1987 ("Arts and the Inner Cities") which was never published because the Department of Environment, or rather the Secretary of State, Nicholas Ridley, objected to its conclusion that local authorities had a key role to play in the artistic life of their communities.

What then can be done? Central government should and could be strengthening the planning laws to incorporate aesthetic criteria. They should be encouraging the use of Section 52 of the Town and Country Planning Act to achieve a better architectural environment, and launching an urgent inquiry into how to promote the Percentage for Art concept in the UK. They should be seriously considering the National Urban Renewal Agency proposals of Rod Hackney, President of the Royal Institute of British Architects, by which £25 billion of investment could be provided over five years for inner city development. Above all, they should be investing in training both at art colleges and at schools of architecture, while supporting artists and craftspeople more actively through the Arts Council, the Regional Arts Associations and through local authorities by means of a statutory responsibility for the arts financed by an earmarked element in the Rate Support Grant. Finally, central government should be setting a better example in its own buildings and public works. When you look at what has been achieved by governments abroad, whether in the underground stations in Stockholm or in the Estate romana policies of Italy in the late 1970s, the potential for exciting initiatives in this country is enormous.

At local government level, there is an equivalent need for most authorities to recognise the importance of these policies and to use more imaginatively the powers that they presently have. In particular, there is an acute need to establish strategic policies in advance of any redevelopment to avoid being led by the nose by private sector developers. When you consider what has been achieved, in projects such as Blackness in Dundee, there is little doubt that we have the artists and architects to transform the quality of our built environment. What we lack is the backing and example of government.

Public art

One way to improve the visual quality of our town centres and public areas is to commission local artists to produce sculptures, murals tapestries, paintings or street decorations which give the town a distinctive feel. It obviously works better if the artists are local because they can reflect local culture and history (often using local materials), and can help provide fresh images and new ideas for local appreciation and debate. Such forms of public art can encourage civic and community pride, a deepening knowledge of local history, as well as directly improving the material environment. They also help support local artists, who may be struggling to get by on very few commissions, encouraging them to stay working in the town.

A recent account of the effectiveness of this kind of public art is to be found in 'Art for Architecture', a lavishly illustrated publication from the Department of Environment. This contains many excellent examples of art used to brighten workplaces, housing estates, airports and stations, town centres and rural parks, and details how the works were commissioned. Many of the artworks shown have made a considerable impact, and there is no doubt that murals and large works of imaginative public sculpture can achieve graphic effects in otherwise ordinary built environments. Thamesdown Borough Council, for example, has developed a strong programme of such art in public places, and with full public consultation. An artists-in-residence programme, supported by Southern Arts, has produced a growing stock of public sculpture in residential areas and shopping centres. In

Swansea, the regeneration of the old docks area into a thriving leisure centre has also included a commitment to local artists' work in public sites.

Planning gains

The hallmark of effective co-operation between local councils and private sector developments should be gains and benefits on both sides. Unfortunately, in the past too many councils gave developers carte blanche over planning permission in return for increased rateable values or the income from land sales. Yet local authorities have powers available to them which can be used for the good of the local community. Section 52 of the Town and Country Planning Act enables councils to make demands in planning agreements for facilities and services to be provided as part of the development package. In Bristol, a development company was happy to provide two arts centres — the Arnolfini and the Watershed — in return for planning permission to develop other sites in the adjacent docks. In Stevenage, a major grocery chain was required to build a community centre and nursery as part of the planning agreement for the development of a new superstore.

However, when it comes to shopping centre development, few local authorities have yet insisted on planning agreements which require, for example, that local retailers be offered premises in the new shopping malls at concessionary rates. As a result, most shopping centre developments insist on rents so high that only the multiples can afford them, and local retailers frequently go out of business. Another solution is that planning permission should only be given for shopping centre developments if a significant percentage of the lettings are made available to independent retailers on a 'turnover rent' basis rather than a high fixed rent.

Another local benefit which should be part of the agreement made with any local authority supplier or developer relates to recruitment and staffing. 'Inner city regeneration' which simply brings in highly paid skilled construction workers from outside to do the work is likely to create considerable resentment. Local labour and equal opportunities clauses are both important conditions for the successful development of joint public/private sector initiatives that also enhance local employment opportunities.

One way for local authorities to retain a measure of control or some influence over what happens in new shopping areas is to employ the mechanism of "contracts compliance". This often relates to equal opportunities policies, particularly the ethnic composition of the workforce or provision of support services for workers with childcare responsibilities, or the rights of workers to join a trade union. This type of good employer contract is far stronger where the local authority is landowner, so that conditions can be written in to leasehold agreements and covenants.

Living in town

As a result of earlier planning policies, residential accommodation was largely moved to the periphery or outskirts of many towns, leaving the centre for shops, offices and services. This has not worked. One of the most important ways of revitalising the town centre in the evening is to create residential accommodation there, so that the town centre has a living community of its own. This was one of the main issues in the Covent Garden planning controversy: the displacement of a large residential population of many generations in favour of offices and shops. As a result of the GLC-backed revitalisation scheme, the residential accommodation in Covent Garden over the past decade has doubled, though this achievement remains under threat.

The 'cultural district'

Many towns and cities lack a 'critical mass' — one place which gives the town a buzz. It may be that in planning to revitalise the evening economy and cultural night-life of a particular place, it is necessary to concentrate provision, where possible, in one district. Hence the notion of the 'cultural quarter' or 'cultural district'. Sheffield is developing just such a sector, immediately south of the main city centre, round the Leadmill Arts Centre and Red Tape Studios, soon to be joined by other elements such as the Sheffield Independent Film Co-operative. Birmingham is considering proposals to establish Digbeth, an area adjoining the old Bull Ring, as a media sector, with a major new media centre and other facilities. At the same time, the general redevelopment of Birmingham's city centre may well see a number of linked open spaces which will contain a wide range of arts and cultural elements convenient for those using the major new Convention Centre.

In many such developments, the arts are acting as a central anchor element. The new concert hall for the City of Birmingham Symphony Orchestra in Birmingham; the restoration of the Alhambra Theatre, and the creation of the National Museum of Photography, Film and Television, in Bradford; the revival of the Burrell Museum in Glasgow; the Merseyside Maritime Museum and the Tate in the North at the Albert Dock in Liverpool; all illustrate the way that major investment in arts projects opens up other possibilities, not least by helping to transform the image of each city.

The conclusion may mistakenly be drawn from this that this role is best, indeed only, fulfilled by the large, capital-intensive, prestige arts project and that community arts activities should be located outside city centres. However, many community arts projects, such as jazz, folk, dance studios, draw audiences and participants from a wide geographic area. Such a mix of arts activities of all scales will have an added benefit of ensuring that city centres, in the evening, are used by people of all ages and income groups.

Buskers and street theatre

Another way of bringing life back into town centres, and also providing employment for local actors and musicians, is to encourage retailers and businesses to fund live performances in the town squares, shopping centres and market places. This has been proved not only to attract business, but also provides artists with a training ground and income necessary for their own development. In Covent Garden the open air entertainment organised by Covent Garden Community Arts has become an established feature of the open square there, and attracts delighted crowds all day long — and in the evening too. For many visitors it is one of the main reasons for going there. A company such as 'No Fit State Circus', whose main income comes from performing in schools, have probably been seen by more people when they've been hired by cities such as Cardiff, Leicester, Southampton and Newcastle-on-Tyne to liven up their shopping precincts.

Signposting

In Britain, signposting within towns is often very poor, leaving visitors (and residents, without many means of finding their way around or to the main public buildings and facilities. Yet bright and bold markers and sign-posts not only tell people where they are and where they might go, they also act as a promotional tool for the facilities themselves. Providing large town maps at the main public gathering points — the railway station, the bus terminus, the post office, the shopping centre, the town square, the market place — together with a comprehensive signposting programme throughout the town will give people a sense of direction and of the choice of facilities available.

Arts and manufacturing

Local designers, arts and craftspeople can also play a key role in the regeneration of the inner city. The Italian experience shows how important such a role can be, especially for small industries like clothing, shoes, tiles, pottery and glass-making. Interesting initiatives of this kind have started in Newcastle-upon-Tyne and Nottingham. Newcastle has created a Fashion Centre based upon the Department of Fashion at the local Polytechnic. Its aim is to increase awareness of the importance of good design among clothing manufacturers in the North East.

Nottingham has launched its 'Frameworks' strategy, which is designed to establish links between the local fashion and textile, audiovisual and microelectronics sectors.

The encouragement of craft workshops and small manufacturing units back into the city centres not only provides jobs but ready-made customers for the products. This corresponds to trends in mainstream retailing, where it is expected that the next wave will be developed around 'inter-active retailing', with customers able to watch their goods being made. The community architecture movement is at the same time reviving the idea of the 'atelier flat' — buildings where people can both live and work.

The importance of the 'integrated approach'

One of the central arguments advanced here is that arts and media policies can contribute effectively to urban regeneration when they are integrated into one single strategy with policies in areas as disparate as transport, policing, housing, planning, childcare, tourism, retailing, employment and economic development.

Transport policy can play a crucial role in opening up the city, and it therefore deserves special mention.

The case for a cheap, efficient, clean, safe, fast and frequent public transport system, running late into the night, can be easily justified. In terms of *social needs*, it increases the mobility of groups such as women, children, young people, the elderly and the poor. In terms of *economic development*, it stimulates a 'round-the-clock' use of the city centre and contributes to the 'doubling' of the city's economy, and in terms of *environmental improvement*, it reduces traffic, noise, pollution, congestion and increases street safety. In a number of cities in the United States, public transport in and around the town centre is totally free, as part of a programme of urban and social renewal.

But, as a result of deregulation and the continuing withdrawal of subsidies, public transport services are in decline. As the table below clearly shows, public transport in many cities in the UK comes bottom of the European list (with the unique exception of Sheffield before deregulation) in terms of government subsidies.

Proportion of public transport costs met by subsidy — 1984/5

City	Percentage
Turin	87
Rome	81
Rotterdam	81
Amsterdam	80
Genoa	79
Sheffield	78
Seattle	70
Athens	70
Bordeaux	70
Miami	69
Los Angeles	69
Antwerp	66
Stockholm	63
Milan	62
Paris	54
London	30

The failure of many governments and local authorities to see the need for efficient and popular public transport programmes as essential to an active town and city life is one of the major reasons for the imbalanced nightmare that urban life has become — with over-crowded streets and congested roads in the daytime, emptiness at night. Yet changes in policy can have quite rapid results, as the GLC showed. In just two years, as a result of cheaper fares, bus use increased by 13%, tube use increased by 44% and car commuting decreased by 21%. The GLC's 'Fair's Fare' campaign was not only popular it was cost-effective too. Unhappily this was quashed by a High Court judgement.

Elsewhere, a number of other local authorities continue to try to develop imaginative responses to the domination of our towns and cities by private cars. The Tyne & Wear Metro, the first rapid light transport system in the UK, and West Yorkshire Passenger Transport Executive's decision to re-introduce trolley bus services in Bradford are two examples. The cheap fares policy of South Yorkshire was eventually supported by all political parties in that region, having demonstrated its effectiveness in creating widespread usage and access. That policy disappeared with the abolition of the Metropolitan County Council and privatisation, and the numbers of journeys taken has dropped considerably.

The need for a comprehensive arts policy at local government level

All of our arguments therefore lead to the centrality of an arts policy as the organising principle of town and city regeneration. But today we have to have a very wide definition of the arts. Therefore below we print a check-list of those kinds of buildings, venues, resources, services and facilities, many if not all of which should now come within the framework of a local arts and cultural industries strategic policy. Not every small town is likely to have everything to hand — but its arts department should at least know where these resources are located locally or regionally.

Art colleges
Arts centres
Artists' materials suppliers
Bookshops (both new and second hand)
Cinemas
Dance studios/training
Design studios
Black and ethnic minority arts provision
Fashion studios/training/education courses
Literary agents
Libraries
Local radio stations
Museums

Music publishers
Music agents
Publishers (local, regional or national)
Provision for the elderly
Pubs with live music
Photographic galleries
Photographic darkrooms and training
Public sculptures
Poetry workshops
Recording studios
Record shops (new and second-hand)
Regional TV stations
Theatres and theatre workshops
Theatrical agents
Technical aid services
Video and television workshops & production
Visual arts galleries
Voluntary organisations: drama, dance, choirs, jazz & rock, orchestras, art & photography, etc.
Writers workshops
Youth provision: dance, drama, music, fashion, design, etc.

This is just a summary list of key services and facilities that added together would provide the outlines of a strategic local 'map' of facilities and services for the whole community.

The importance of public consultation

Any local authority strategy for regeneration should start from a process of the widest public consultation and a survey of those organisations and resources which already exist. Too many local authorities adopt a stand-offish relationship with both the 'voluntary sector' in arts and environmental provision and with the private sector. Such surveys could usefully include information on the scale, frequency and time that people use existing arts facilities; where they come from; by what means of transport; and what else they combine with their arts activities. Such wider information will lead inevitably on to a consideration of related services such as bars, pubs, restaurants, clubs and hotels, and raises questions of licensing policy and policing, along with more obvious implications for transport and housing. Quantitative surveys may well also need to be augmented by more detailed reports from professional consultancies which analyse a particular market. COMEDIA, for example, have recently completed just such a report for

Birmingham on the potential for the audio-visual industry in that city. Only when armed with this type of information will local authorities be in a position properly to address the central questions of what is the role, function and contribution of the arts in the economic and cultural life of our city centre.

Not all strategic arts policy-making necessarily involves large amounts of expenditure; some of the most effective arts policies have been based as much on the efficient exchange of information as on straightforward grants.

Merseyside County Council produced an excellent directory, 'Arts on Merseyside', in 1986, which listed all arts organisations, performers, venues, services, equipment, training facilities and resources, and this model could be widely adopted elsewhere.

At the same time, local arts bodies should be encouraged to produce public statements of their aims and objectives, asked to identify their key audiences, and to examine whether they are reaching the people they really want to. The opinions of the widest possible range of local voluntary organisations — not just the artistic ones — should also be sought on what kind of arts, leisure and town centre provision they would like. Out of such processes of consultation can come a local arts strategy that is based on consultation rather than received tradition. Of course, people should be made aware of the likely cost, and encouraged to make informed priorities and choices. Oxford City Council, for example, when running a programme of leisure development on one of its larger council estates, circulated to each house a questionnaire about what facilities people would like to see in their locality. But it also costed each item and asked people to bear costings in mind when choosing priorities (i.e. spend the whole budget on two big super facilities or spread the money around on a wider range of community provision). The more people are involved the greater the loyalty they will feel to the services provided.

The consultation process can also be important to raise public aesthetic awareness of the urban environment. Some US cities have successfully established municipal Design Review Boards involving councillors, relevant professionals (planners, architects, visual artists) and local citizens. Their duty is to monitor changes in the city centre's physical environment, to suggest ways of making it more effective and to promote design awareness programmes.

The Way Forward: making the case for investment in the arts

It has often been very difficult in the past to make the case for spending on 'the arts'. The arts have been seen as 'middle class', marginal, elitist, 'wet', escapist, diversionary, potentially scandalous, or dismissed with some other contemptible phrase. Hence a tiny budget, a lowly place in the local government committee structure, a few crumbs handed out after the 'serious' local government services have taken their share of the budget. In fact, for too long we have made the wrong arguments. The arts are not a piece of decoration or a luxury, but at the centre of the major cultural industries of our time. The case that should be made today is that investment in training, in the arts as a major sector for job creation and economic development, can release new sources of money at local authority level. It can win funds and other resources from local industry and the private sector, can win planning gains in housing and retail development, and can be an economic and strategic key to urban reconstruction. But the future of our city centres, and the role that the arts play there, will depend significantly on who gains control of development policies — central government, local authorities, or the private developers.

The present government is in no doubt that the key partnership should be between itself and the private sector. It points to the success of American cities like Baltimore, where private capital in the Inner Harbor scheme has been stimulated by Urban Development Action Grants. This has been the model for the UK government's original seven Urban Development Corporations, to which six more have now been added. In particular, the government would take credit for the Merseyside UDC, with key cultural investments in the renovation of the Albert Dock and the creation of the Tate in the North.

It is possible even that the Government might claim that the UDCs are an improvement on the American Action Grants, which involve no audit provisions and which do not require developers to justify their applications for grants. However, such arguments ignore the fact that in the United States, it is local government which controls economic development policy; which can adjust land values on public land; can abate taxes on property; raise subsidised capital for loans; control its own job training programmes; and, above all, which has the power to borrow or to raise its own taxes without expenditure limits or rate caps.

But if the present government, through the UDCs, is determined to avoid the involvement of local authorities, those same local councils are equally insistent that they should be involved. Authorities like Glasgow, Sheffield, Newcastle and Birmingham recognise, however, that successful development is going to depend on a partnership between themselves, the private sector, the general public, central government, and other agencies, although the precise relationships will vary in each case. Bradford provides a good example of this, with central government investment in the National Museum of Photography, Film and Television, and private sector capital in Salt's Mill and the central retail development, both augmenting the contribution of the Arts Council (in London Festival Ballet's five-year relationship with the Alhambra) and the Victoria and Albert Museum's proposed siting of part of its Indian sub-continent collection in Salt's Mill. All of this investment has been made possible by pump-priming initiatives from the City council.

The resolution of this central issue of the relative roles of central and local government will be crucial in determining the type, scale and quality of the regeneration of city centres. What is certain is that, vital though private investment is, the developers cannot revive city centres by themselves. Even in the deregulated world of the UDCs, there is need for co-operation with the neighbouring local authorities on the essential infrastructure of transport, refuse, policing and licensing. Indeed, the more forward-looking management of UDCs, as in the Lower Don Valley, Sheffield, know that they can benefit considerably from working closely with the City Council.

It is also the case that, whatever the balance, there will be a need for a major input from central government, by means of enabling legislation and, above all, capital investment. No solution to the revival of our city centres can be cost free for the general taxpayer, nor should it be.

But in our view, revival cannot simply be imposed from Whitehall. The Office of Arts and Libraries report "Arts and the Inner Cities" makes it clear that, whatever the equation, the role of the local authorities is essential. Without it, investment will inevitably be imposed on a city from on high and it will prove difficult, if not impossible, to integrate with the existing relationships and expectations of communities. Such problems may already be emerging in Liverpool, where the Albert Dock development, containing the Tate in the North and the Merseyside Maritime Museum, has been parachuted onto the local economy and has few points of contact with the individual artists in Liverpool or with the existing arts community. Without such integration, there is a danger that it will become a focus for the growing Liverpool tourist industry rather than for local people.

Even if the means exist to develop such strategic planning, there is still an urgent need for local authorities to rethink and redefine both the role that the arts and cultural industries play in their local economies and their communities, and the role that their city centre plays in that wider arts policy. The first step in such rethinking may be to reconsider what is meant by the arts, and to widen definitions beyond the performing and fine arts, crafts, museums, galleries and libraries, to include broadcasting; film, video and photography; publishing; the music and record industries; design; fashion; architecture; and the industries which service these such as retail, laboratories, hire equipment, consultancies. Implicit in this wider definition is the fact that the arts and cultural industries are located as much in the independent, commercial sector as in the public.

If the arts are to play their full part, then, in the revitalisation of our towns and cities, they will need to be at the centre of new strategic policy structures and resources. Cross-committee and cross-departmental teams may be necessary, combining the experience, expertise and strategic planning of economic development, arts and leisure, planning, tourism, policing, education, highways and engineering services, and so on. Some people have recommended the establishment of a Town Centre Committee, appointing a Town Centre Manager to liaise with the private retailing sector and other companies to bring about a joint programme of investment and action. These choices will be different from town to town. But they are likely to be necessary.

For thousands of years the city has been at the centre of social and cultural development throughout the world. It is time it became the centre of our local government strategic planning too. For years we have not seen the wood for the trees, as each separate local government department has gone its own way. The alternative to the rediscovery and nurturing of a strong civic culture is the increased privatisation of social life behind closed doors in suburban housing estates, and the city and the town centre left (after the shops have closed) to skate-boarders, security dogs and the new urban homeless. That is the case put at its most graphic. But it represents the choices which have to be made.

The centres of our great cities are the focus of life for the majority of people, they form the main locations for this country's economic, commercial and social activity. If they thrive, Britain thrives. We cannot afford to let them wither away.

Further Reading

Below is an introductory list of books which further develop the ideas in this pamphlet:

Art for Architecture, Deanna Petherbridge (ed.), HMSO, 1987

Art in Public Places, John Beardsley, Partners for Livable Places, Washington, 1981

Art — Who Needs It?, Lewis, Morley & Southwood, Comedia, 1987

Making Space: Women and the Man Made Environment, Matrix, Pluto Press, 1987

Cities with a Future, Ken Baynes, Design Council in association with Channel 4, 1987

The City as a Stage, K.W. Green (ed.), Partners for Livable Places, Washington, 1983

Community Architecture: How people are creating their own environment, Nick Wates & Charles Knevitt, Penguin Books, 1987

Cultural Facilities in Mixed-Use Development, Harold Snedcof (ed.), The Urban Land Institute, Washington, 1985

Facts about the Arts 2, John Myerscough, Policy Studies Institute, 1986

Getting There: A Transport Policy, Friends of the Earth, 1987

Help for the High Street: Some New Approaches to Revitalisation, Dr. R.L. Davies, Tesco PLC, 1987

The Heritage Industry, Robert Hewison, Methuen, London, 1987

Leisure Industries — An Overview, C. Gratton & P. Taylor, Comedia, 1987

Let's Build a Monument, Theo Crosby, Pentagram Design, London, 1987

'Living for the City', Franco Bianchini, New Socialist, April 1987

Local Government and the Arts, Luisa Kreisbergs (ed.), American Council for the Arts, New York, 1979.

Man Made the Town, Michael Middleton, Bodley Head, 1987.

On the Town: A Strategy for Leisure & Choice, SEEDS, 1987

Out of Town Retail Developments: The need for a planning strategy, National Chamber of Trade, 1987, **Out of Town Shopping Centres:** Some Key Questions, Southampton City Council, 1987

People & Planning (The Skeffington Report), HMSO, 1969

The Phoenix Partnership, Urban Regeneration in the 21st Century, Harry Cowie, National Council for Building Material Producers, London, 1985

Place Makers: Public Art That Tells You Where You Are, Ronald Lee Fleming & Renata Von Tscharner, Hastings House, New York, 1981

Saturday Night or Sunday Morning?, Geoff Mulgan & Ken Worpole, Comedia, 1986.

Streets Ahead, Design Council and the Royal Town Planning Institute, Design Council, London, 1979

Trade Winds: The Changing Face of Retail and Retail Employment in the South East, SEEDS, 1987

Recommendations for Further Action by Local Authorities:

Consultation

1. Surveys to find out what people want, need or are concerned about. These should be designed to target the needs and views of women, young people, the elderly and retired people, people with disabilities, ethnic minorities, non-car owners, town centre residents as well as shoppers and town centre employees.

2. A town centre forum, perhaps serviced by its own secretariat, comprising members from the retail community, councillors and local government officers, local arts groups, trade unions, restaurant owners, publicans, library and museum managers, the police, market traders, transport workers, taxi-drivers, local property developers and sympathetic pension fund managers. This body would devise a town centre strategy. The approach could be extended to cover local shopping districts and civic centres as well as town centres.

Structural Renewal & the Built Environment

3. Improvements to existing buildings and environment rather than extra full-blown property development schemes.
4. Development of new space, well designed from accessibility as well as aesthetic point of view.
5. More flexible use of existing spaces, eg. shopping malls as concert venues, pedestrian areas for semi-permanent street theatre, use of portable venues such as urban tents for rock concerts, circuses, large scale video screenings of films, rock concerts, operas, football matches.
6. More buildings to be used for informal as well as formal leisure, eg. development of sports centre and leisure centre cafes and bars, cafes in museums.
7. Popular planning and design for key sites, along the lines of the GLC's Coin Street model.
8. More town centre housing (at reasonable rents/prices) and conversion of empty town centre office spaces into residential accommodation.
9. Development of percentage for art schemes.
10. Rest areas, creches, supervised play areas, landscaping, well-maintained toilets, i.e. development of civic facilities for local users, customers, retail employees, more parks and public areas open later at night — and well lit.
11. Consult with police, women's groups, organisations for the elderly regarding public safety. Also involve providers of public transport and night-time forms of recreation and leisure with a view to improving mobility and safety at night.
12. Greater use of Section 52 planning gains for development of public facilities.

Cultural Initiatives

13. More attention to the quality of street design and furniture.
14. Development of a public arts policy resculptures, murals, water gardens, etc.
15. Encouragement of buskers and street theatre.
16. Focal events such as light shows, firework displays in town centre, festivals, fairs, open days at the local theatre, concert hall, museum, arts centre.
17. Promote public art (environmental sculpture, murals, mosaics, fountains and other water-based constructions, other 'place-

makers') to make the city centres more special and strengthen local identity.

18. Provide large town maps at the main public gathering places.
19. Undertake comprehensive review of architectural lighting and of the colour of the buildings and streets. Wherever necessary, widen the town's chromatic range through extensive repainting, planting and flower schemes, multi-coloured awnings, etc.
20. Development of a youth cultural economy around recording studios, independent record labels, film and video, dance, fashion and design — and local retailing.
21. Crafts and design workshops, especially those working with local materials and establishing or revitalising local industries.
22. Development of cultural districts or cultural quarters where restaurants, pub theatres, cinemas, dance studios, live music venues are encouraged to open or re-locate to, in order to achieve a 'critical mass' of evening activities that make a place feel alive.
23. Develop a strategy aimed at stimulating the 'evening economy' in the town/city centre, by offering residents and visitors a wide choice of shops, eating and drinking venues and places of entertainment that are open in the evening.

Supporting Public Services

24. Regular street cleaning, anti-litter drive, fines for dog shit.
25. Greater and more sensitive policing at night, protection of people rather than 'fire brigade' policing.
26. Cheap, fast, reliable, frequent, flexible and secure late night public transport.
27. Transport policy to balance needs of public and the car, eg. Park and Ride in Oxford and Brighton.

Retail Policy

28. Strategic policy required setting limits on and locations of out-of-town stores.
29. Rental policies to retain food stores and local retailers, specialist shops, start-up retailers.
30. Co-ordination of deliveries, distribution and agreement on transport policies.
31. A system of grants and loans to independents to improve physical condition and accessibility of shops, in return for agreement on employment conditions, health and safety at work, etc.
32. Greater control over ugly and inappropriate shopfronts.

33. Positive use of markets as points of attraction.
34. Local retail employment training plans to improve quality of training and extend career opportunities to women and ethnic minorities.
35. Local pre-entry package for people considering setting up in retail business.
36. Partnership improvement schemes with major UK retail multiples and property investment institutions.

Central Government Policy

37. Improve planning laws to include greater consideration of aesthetics (eg. shopfronts, high-rise, short-life retail warehouses, etc.)
38. Commission inquiry into the town centre effects of the retail revolution.
39. Endorse Percentage for Art scheme.
40. Cancel Urban Development Corporations and Enterprise Zones, in favour of local government/private sector based joint initiatives.
41. Improve training for architects, and include greater provision for community architecture.
42. Set better standards for public buildings and remaining public utilities, eg. post offices, DHSS buildings, railway stations.
43. Unified Ministry for the Arts & Media.
44. Ministerial responsibility for retailing.